As for Love

AS FOR LOVE
Poems & Translations

M. L. Rosenthal

New York   Oxford
OXFORD UNIVERSITY PRESS
1987

Oxford University Press

Oxford   New York   Toronto
Delhi   Bombay   Calcutta   Madras   Karachi
Petaling Jaya   Singapore   Hong Kong   Tokyo
Nairobi   Dar es Salaam   Cape Town
Melbourne   Auckland

and associated companies in
Beirut   Berlin   Ibadan   Nicosia

Copyright © 1987 by M. L. Rosenthal

Published by Oxford University Press, Inc.,
200 Madison Avenue, New York, New York 10016

Oxford is a registered trademark of Oxford University Press

Library of Congress Cataloging-in-Publication Data

Rosenthal, M. L. (Macha Louis), 1917-
    As for love
I. Foix, J.V.   Poems.   English.   1987.   II. Title
P.S.3568.O84A9   1987   811'.52   87-18468
ISBN 0-19-504969-1
ISBN 0-19-505268-4 (pbk.)

2 4 6 8 10 9 7 5 3 1
Printed in the United States of America
on acid-free paper

Grateful acknowledgment is made to the following publications in which many of these poems appeared in their original form: *Agenda* (London), *American Poetry Review, Eidos, Forbes, Georgia Review, Ohio Wesleyan Literary Review* (*Owl*), *Open Places, Parnassus, Pequod, The Poetry Review, Present Tense, Southern Review, Translation*. I am deeply indebted as well to the late J. V. Foix for his permission to publish translations of his poems from the Catalan.

CONTENTS

Invocation

I AS FOR LOVE

II A CHOICE OF TITLES

III THE BLONDE ON THE BEACH

INVOCATION
(for V. H. R.)

Never to be carved on time's tall cenotaph,
forgotten names mass in the icy flatlands
(mind's tundra, waste-world of lost heritage):
vanished shadows whispering in vanished tongues.
And even our remembered, long-wept, dearest dead
must helpless, on Erebus' darker side, await
a day by hope foretold, by God withheld.

Guard bravely the living, O earthbound presences
of mirth, sweet memory, desire. Guard well
the delicate tracings of small faces; guard
the piping hubris of baby throats. Hold firm
where dangers lurk: the threshold, the thronging street,
the gentle thoughts of those I love, and all
our fragile, suffering, passionate, murdering race.

I

As for Love

AS FOR LOVE

I
Water Lilies, White Violets

So close to the grass as I ran—
over white violets!—
and then the springy swamp
and then the water lilies—
                    cool blooms
of warm-wet June.

                    A sleeping infant, babe of the stars,
holds a roomful of men and women in thrall:
the distance, untouchable distance,
and delicate persistence
light years away, in the sway
of the streaming hours.

                    No redress, my darling,
only love's baby dream, untouchable, innocent,
till we return where water lilies made us smile
and find
          a quarrel, or reproach,
some industrial park where spawning marshes were.

The floating clouds were creviced, careless, rosy.
You could not see the blood of slaughtered villages—
only the sunset float of white violets in a meadow,
only the float of baby blankets in the sky,
each with its folded, sleeping message.

II

Dissolving Mirror

| LEARN | LIVE | NO | LOVE |

When I am young and handsome again
I shall remember narrow lanes, and rain,
old loves, names of the dead,
earth-smells, grass-smells, Mr. Worms
the gardener, twang of tennis racquets,
Miriam, or Eva, at twilight, gravely
speaking. Hungarian Johnny
will be waiting to fight me once again.
Winter sunlight on a sled piled with books . . .
I shall find you somewhere there
in the dissolving mirror.

In what city, where
shall I meet you in the old shy way?
What name will you be wearing?
An old man with beautiful eyes told me a tale
of narrow lanes, in Souzhow, in the rain,
where whores and flower-girls cried their wares
and graybeards begged for bread near every door.
The nights were misty then, in the old China,
and I, so young and handsome then,
would walk the endless lanes and kiss
my phantom loves into sad poems.

The old songs will come drifting up.
"The young folks roll on the little cabin floor"
while their elders argue politics. She will watch
from her window again, watch for her son. Earth's old
dark round . . .

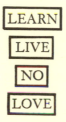

                  . . . Oh, but here's a lucky
crossroads! Here's a loving girl! Here's
a young and handsome again fellow,
able and willing, shouting into the mirror,
inviting you out:
                 Come and lovely swim
with me, quick, before the weather changes.

III

As for Love

A distraction from the wars. Or a grove,
where ardent spirits mingle . . . The rain
outside the window tonight, the work
always fruitful, always giving birth
to more work, and more. Brute sorrow
gulps down one more long night, ravening
for the coming long whole day. And
"Are you not weary of ardent ways?" I

shall never be—no, not even while
these miracles flow on: the green valley
that became a cliff; the clear stream
that became a bourgeois affair and stopped
wherever the little angels go
for their little breakfasts and to
get away from it all. (And tell them:
"Eat hearty, little angels. The brute

will feed on you when ready, and never—
will never choke on your sweet
little ardent ways, never grow weary
of edible laughter and sunlight
and love that rises in mist, crystallizes
into cliffs, and exactly at dawn will fix
one granite eye on ardent ways.") Gently
past all this, O life, let me hold my love.

IV
Since the Moment Arrived

Since the moment arrived I have believed in the death
that neither my father's nor my mother's had proved to me.
Although once, long ago, I did lurch through the Gate,
it was but a misstep into eternal space,
a wrong turning. Once, too, in the Villa Borghese,
I found myself on a path along the high ridge
lined by hovels and tiny vegetable patches.
Poverty stank there, above the noble view of Rome.

Now crocuses, daffodils, the returning robin,
a growth that won't go away, a recurrent bleeding,
a sudden fatigue, terror of the moon's face,
stupor that smothers the lingering stab of pain,
dark stagnant water under the ancient Souzhow bridges,
death's-heads of cyclists soaring into the dawn—
I accept, accept, accept what's now imaginable.

What was it I dreamt? Two imperial swans
eternal in the lagoon of the Emperor's palace grounds,
swimming proudly, glorious pair, below, above, the moon-glow.

V
Farewell without Leaving

Farewell, without leaving. The changing
seasons hold. Memory, monster, supple
old man, woman, of the sea, under
the water, earth, years,
you.

      Why, yet again,
those black horses a-gallop in a heat-shimmering sky?
Why, again, her voice thrilling with joy? those burning-red
barbtoothed fish, thrashing
in pitching seas of golden meadow?

                      Sudden
the pitch-black rectangle blazes. Inside,
on the bed, bright splash of red
on a dead-white face. Gold blouse,
green skirt. She lies back, pulls
the green up over gleaming thighs.
Memory framed these fifty years.

                     And
"Ich vill nit shtarbn!" I hear
your scream, poor lady, all the long night piercing
my pubescent solitude. Step-aunt, my mother's burden,
in cancer's pincer-grip, in the next room to mine.

Sunrise a spinning, grinning crab, the whole morning
swinging helpless from his claw. "I *won't* die!"

Goodbye,

goodbye without leaving, at dawn.

VI

The Rose of Love and the Lotus

We shall not meet where mazes end.
Love flows underground and reappears
in memory's interstices perhaps while you
are hurrying elsewhere. And then was then.

The rose of love and the lotus
may careless bloom, with praises warm, again
till slowly, slowly, sunlight melts the prison-locks.

Till the brain's no longer a prison?

The brain no longer a prison.

Tired of sorrow, old cliché that barks.
Weary of the ages. Round Shanghai faces
sullen at dusk, feral glow of old moons . . .
Ten million cyclists riding into dawn,
just going to work, and then I lose count.
China, I sing your ancient misery and wisdom!
Ten million cyclists ride into dawn—and then
I lose count.
                    That's China for you, first thing in the morning.
And last thing at night there's nothing, save
one billion sleeping souls, and all the rice
in China.

(How slow life was. Nomads, villages, rain, grain.
Rice-dance, rice-song, rice-prayer, rice-tax.
Let the child be a son. Let the monkey-king
and the concubines and the fat little godlets thrive.
Let the arrogant noble make ink for the drunken poet.)

No longer a prison.

We talked at happy ease—
innocent, pleasing phrases
(dreams could not be better)
without care, warm with praises.
So would I have it be again.

    When I begged for bread in doorways
    invisible to flower-girl and whore
    took my crusts from thrusting hands
    my eyes rain-blurred even in clear sunlight
    my wordless mumble wet rust on old chains
    my smell of piss and incense
    beard of stained hay-wisps
    memory a worn drumskin
    sharp-flicked by voice-whips eye-whips
    woman-eyes unseeing juggernaut-male voices
    slick paving stones of old Souzhow
    sleeping begging weeping
              guarding the rose and the lotus.

VII
White Lotus, Pink Lotus

A little clearing, a breathing space. Then
down one gentle step
from yesterday. Then
down one other.
Downward's so gentle.
Upward's so steep.

Red sunset on the water.

She turned resolutely, like a figure in a poem,
like a figure in a window, like a figure in a garden.

Cast thy bread, and
give love, and
watch it go
where the spring goes
and the autumn, summer, winter
and the vows, the caresses, the sweet aftertimes.

On the slow, underwater streams
lost lovers floating, faces down.

*   *   *

We are not unique.
We are not even we.
I bequeath what I never possessed
to the days and nights as they flow
from my fingers and away.

The lotus is in bloom,
white, pink.
The faces have turned upward.
Red sheen on black depths.
The faces open upward.

VIII
Year's End

Thin wind of loneliness
cold as this December night.

                      Poor love,

the grave's lonely, I know.
What made you think I'd forgotten?

SOUZHOW LANES IN THE RAIN
(*from the Chinese of Zhao Ruihong*)

A misty, drizzling autumn evening:
under my dark red oilpaper umbrella, trimmed in black,
I wander the Souzhow lanes in the rain
from one to another, from one to another.

On the long winding flagstone lanes
my footsteps echo: hypnotic music.
River and bridge give shape to this beauty,
a kind of heaven between whitewashed walls.

Raindrops patter on my oilpaper umbrella
and on the smooth, clean, far-reaching flagstones.
I wander here, wander there;
this famed old city speaks a poem all her own.

Tonight I see no girl with tear-brimming eyes,
selling smiles mixed with sighs, like sad violets,
trudging the long-stretching lanes in the rain:
lanes as endless, to her, as the tale of her grief.

(Nowadays she might be a splendid weaver of silk,
whole bolts of it streaming in every brave color—
and flamboyant brocades and shining satin,
admired for her skills by all her companions.)

Tonight I find no flower-girl near the whitewashed wall
calling her wares—"Jasmine! Gardenias!"—
with quavering voice and hungry eyes,
laden with more sorrows by far than flowers.

(Nowadays you'd find her, maybe, in a flower-commune,
distilling lovely perfumes—"Jasmine! Gardenias!"—
and sipping lingjing tea with its fragrance of roses
as she gazes out over the fields turning golden.)

Tonight I meet no beggar, hardly alive,
scrounging for scraps at door after door,
cold raindrops glistening on his silvery hair,
the wailing wind his one cruel comrade.

(Nowadays he'd be snug enough—his own place to stay,
chatting in the lamplight, playing chess under the trees.
And who knows? He might have a son, a noted geologist,
who leaves his firm footprint on both sides of the Yangtze.)

Raindrops patter on my oilpaper umbrella
and on the smooth, clean, far-reaching flagstones.
I wander here, wander there,
and listen to the music of old and new Souzhow.

Noisy workshops and falling rain make a chorus,
lights are bright in each house I pass,
a girl is calling, "Let's go hear the singers!"
and sweet scents from courtyards drift through the lanes.

A misty, drizzling autumn evening:
under my dark red oilpaper umbrella, trimmed in black,
I wander the Souzhow lanes in the rain,
from one to another, from one to another.

II

A Choice of Titles

A CHOICE OF TITLES

(1) "LET US REMEMBER"; (2) "IN HUMILIATION"; (3) "I NO LONGER DESIRE YOU"; (4) "THIS DAY"; (5) "WHAT A RIDICULOUS LOVE"; (6) "THE CRICKETS ARE SINGING"; (7) "COME THROUGH THE NIGHT ON THE WIND OF FORGETTING"

"Violence in Bethlehem today, as
Christians prepared for Easter and Jews
prepared for Passover. A bomb exploded
in Manger Street. No one was injured."

Putting one and one together, old God,
cautious poker player, said "Check
to the dealer"—old Fate, who (naturally)
passed. Both folded. And then Fate told
what she considered a droll tale, viz:

"This man was strolling along, when suddenly
he realized (having lavished You know
how much time and moolah on his mistresses)
that in bed and out his wife had, always,
brought him more bliss than the whole bunch
of them together. He saw it bright
and clear. What a catastrophe! The waste!"

Ruthlessly but hardly toothlessly, the "golden
laughter" of old God and old Fate rang out.
"I heard that broadcast," old God chuckled;
"how come 'no one was injured'?" "You can't
win 'em all," whinnied old Fate, "hee-heeee!"

"Foreseeing executions, the turmoil of murderous events,
I decamped to the nereids on the shores of the Black Sea."

Let us remember the song of the crickets
and the famous tales of undying love—aye,
thine and mine, cloud-dwelling love—
and God's love for the world and the peoples,
glints of cosmic dust, divine resonances
we, the undesired and forgotten, do not believe.
Let us remember the song of the crickets,
remember and set our faces hard against the truth.

On a night (such a night!)
the crickets were singing, singing,
oh, the crickets were singing
the only song they knew in the world:

"I no longer   desire you"
"I no longer   desire you"
"I no longer   desire you"
"I no longer   desire you"
"I no longer   desire you"

Let us remember the song of the crickets,
O come through the night on the wind of forgetting
yet remember. What a ridiculous love.
The heart   pumps   only   blood;
in humiliation stops, when
denied oxygen; on that day (this day)

cares less than old Fate, or old God,
whether its container loves or is loved.

   "I no longer   desire you"

      (*Fate:* Did you catch the punch line?
      God: Yes. He—it—said "Desire you."
      Fate: They said "I no longer   desire you."
      God: So, the crickets no longer desire you?
      Fate: Old Imbecile, that's not what it means!
      God: I've read those lines of Mandelstam's. How come
         the nereids didn't save him, then?
      Fate: You can't lose 'em all either—wheee-heee!)

Exeunt Fate and God, thwacking each other's bottoms
   with rubber bladders.

GOLDEN THOUGHTS

"Pile the bodies high at Austerlitz"—
    so one poet wrote, recalling great Napoleon.
        Wasn't that a fair field full of folk, though,
            made fertile for money?

And at Auschwitz later, they piled 'em up too,
    pulled out the gold fillings. Where are (*ach, wo?*)
        those gold fillings now? And:
            "We took the gold and left the Spaniard lying"—Drake's

blood-thick Anglo-Saxon sword-wit. One thought
    surely begets another. I remember
        my mother sifting ashes (if you catch the drift)
            for want of money, money, money . . . and

those swollen-bellied Biafran babies, black
    as the oil they died for. But what the hell
        do poets, dreaming of Atlas' daughters hiding
        in Taurus' burning bosom, hiding

from Orion (his great blue blazing eye, and
    his great red blazing eye) know about money?
        Only what Mallarmé said:
        "One throw of the dice

will never change
    the nature of chance." Rich folks
        have it, poor folks lack it,
            most are in the latter bracket.

But honey, what do poets know about money?

DANSES MACABRES
(*usual skeletal chorus*)

Mafioso, hijack goon,
heads of state in name or fact,
NATO and the Warsaw Pact
all are whirling to one tune:
    Change your partners, swing around
    and shoot-shoot-shoot with a bang-bang sound.

Moslem, Christian, atheist, Jew,
Buddhist, Shiite, Sikh, Hindu,
I.R.A. gunman, Orangeman too
all know exactly what to do:
    Change your partners, swing around
    and shoot-shoot-shoot with a bang-bang sound.

Who calls the shots? Just ask the guns.
Who pays the piper? Ask the guns.
Who knows the reasons? Ask the guns.
And who's the winner? Ask the guns.
    Change your partners, swing around
    and shoot-shoot-shoot with a bang-bang sound.

And there's a *danse* for skinny folk
jerked up, jerked down on puppet-strands
in El Salvador and other lands
where fear (like pity)'s a dirty joke:
    Run here, hide there, swing around
    and jump-jump-jump to the bang-bang sound.

SIX TITLES FOR SONGS OF THE BALKAN PEOPLES

(1)

"Come Back to Me Dead or Not at All" ("Maiden's Song," from *Yashlak Stood at the Point Where the Four Swords Meet*)

(2)

"They Tried to Storm Our Village, but They Couldn't Find It" (from *Brave Starovak Drank Them All Under*)

(3)

"We Cut Down the Albanians with Hammer-Blows from Our Rifles" (from *Idylls of Lake Ochrid*)

(4)

"Say, What Do You Think You Are, Anyway, Foolish Fellow?" (from *Zhvotno Held Fast Against the Croatians*)

(5)

"The Lover's Reply to the Bandits" (from *Who Steals My Trash May Have Her, and Also My Good Name, but Don't Insult My Fatherland*)

(6)

"They Called Him a Coward, but He Killed the Whole Village" (from Stazhnak Cvetznik's translation of Oliver Goldsmith's "The Deserted Village," adapted for the Macedonian Folk Festival Cycle of Traditional Peasant Songs of All Nations)

THE BALLAD OF THE SAD DYBBUK

Yankel Schmybbuk met a dybbuk
Singin' on the street.
Says Yankel Schmybbuk to the dybbuk,
"What makes you sing so sweet?"

Says the dybbuk to Yankel Schmybbuk,
"Love's sweeter than a *briss*.*
Yankel Schmybbuk or a dybbuk—
Love *schmiers* you with a kiss.

"When Yenta Schmenta I did enta
My corpse and I were through.
I meanta enta Yenta Schmenta
And tormenta black-and-blue.

"When Yenta Schmenta I did enta
My voice could crack concrete.
But Yenta Schmenta's creamy centa
Turned my *croak* to *tweet-tweet-tweet*.

"The exorcist who x'd my bliss
Balked my demonic glory.
So here I linga till I. B. Singa
Finds me and tells my story.

"Oi, here I'll linga till I. B. Singa
Comes along and takes my part.
For I. B. Singa will certainly linga
O'er a dybbuk's broken heart."

* Circumcision ritual

NO SECOND LIFE

The door shuts. And, from the window, I
regard the street and, God knows why,
wait for something terribly sweet
(as the idiom goes) to return to me.

Eternal wait! my song let rise in time
but such a time as never measure had,
clockless, wandering, dreamless: memory
held pure forever, gay and sad.

"Forever," word fluttering in space,
mind's torment, aphrodisiac:
I see you dimly as the sky turns black—
Shekinah, woman without a face.

SEVEN POEMS BY J. V. FOIX
(*from the Catalan*)

FOUR SONNETS

I

Alone, in mourning, wearing an archaic black gown,
I stray often into dark solitudes,
Uncharted plains where high slate-mounds surround
Me, and everywhere I'm blocked by ocean-deep whirlpools.

And I ask: Where's this? for what antique grounds,
What dead skies or pastures long mute
Are you headed, maniac? toward what never-to-be-found
Miraculous star do you beat onward heavy-footed?

Alone I'm immortal. Palpable in that landscape
Of a thousand years back, strangeness isn't strange to me:
I know myself at home; parched deserts can't derange me

Or the coldest snowcapped peaks. I've got my lands back safe
Just where I used to wander: in the live-trap God arranged for me.
Or the one the Devil made Him; in exchange for me.

II

It pleases me, when the fancy strikes, to meander by walls
Still standing from antique times, and as dusk comes on
To dream, under some laurel near some crude fountain,
With my eyes almost shut, of old sieges and battles.

It pleases me, mornings, to pick up my pliers and other tools
And get to work and tighten some snug-fitting pin
So the gear will mesh just right, or adjust a bushing that cushions
An axle, and then purr out with smooth power over the asphalt

And snake up and down mountain-passes, towards valleys in shadow,
And ford streams in a furious rush: Ah, a new world!
Also, these things are pleasing: a linden tree's gentle shade,

A museum of antiquities, madonnas turning dark and fading,
And the far-out stuff of our painters nowadays! I'm a child:
Everything new thrills and exalts me, and I'm mad for everything old.

III

I'm afraid at night, yet meanwhile night carries me away
Paralyzed, down back alleys, along the sea brackish with soot;
A makeshift, out-of-tune band plays somewhere in the dying light,
And I'm by myself, all alone, and that's a comfort certainly.

Black slag-heaps loom up all around the dead sea,
And the flattened hill, and the pine-clump tonight,
But I peer deep and spy a lush woods in their midst,
And imagine a doorway in the wasteland where it can't be.

Suddenly I see: the pitch-dark night's a huge blackboard,
And, like a kid, I start drawing funny faces and noses,
And the new world, the promised land we've always desired.

I gape, I'm afraid—oh night that isolates naked and pure
Stars and wisdom! You fill the whole sea with cast-off clothes,
And I hear a voice saying: "Blood's raining into the cisterns."

IV

If I could match Reason to Madness exactly,
And one bright morning, close to the bright sea,
If my spirit, so very greedy for joy,
Could touch the Eternal then and there! If fantasy

—That my heart sets on fire and my misery turns away—
Could just at will, by word, sound, and melody,
Make today hold forever; and if my shadow, mysteriously
Mocking me from walls, would teach and guide me

As I walk among the tamarisks and gravestones
—Oh sweet reverie! sweet taste in my mouth!—
My purloined hopes would prove true, and in secret zones

The images that my eyes in sleep summon forth
Would come alive, time would cease, and for once
The long-dreamt Immortals would glow here and dance!

1913–27

IT WAS GROWING DARK AND WE STARED AT THE HIDES SCATTERED ABOUT THE SADDLER'S HOUSE

Already vapors enfold the gardens;
Roots draw back into mystery, in earth and in walls—
All the mock skins of things, now forgotten,
Lost in the deep sandpits of the night.
Friendly, we cede them to the deceitful hour.
Aroused and nervous, herds of mares
Born in shadow and nourished by shadow
Reach the tiny hamlets.
High above the elephant pelt of the sky
The stars open out their airy pathways.

April 1928

IT'S WHEN I SLEEP THAT I SEE CLEARLY

It's when it rains that I dance by myself
All dressed up in algae, gold, and fish-scales.
There's a stretch of sea just around the bend
And a nice patch of scarlet sky,
A bird whirls a perfect pirouette
And a bush preens with new branches,
The pirate's hideaway castle
Is an enormous sunflower.
It's when it rains that I dance by myself
All dressed up in algae, gold, and fish-scales.

It's when I laugh that I seem hunchbacked
In the pool just under the threshing-floor.
Disguised as an aging gent
I start chasing the caretaker's wife,
And between the pine-tree and the oak
Is where I plant my banner;
And brandishing my awl
I slay the unnameable monster.
It's when I laugh that I seem hunchbacked
In the pool just under the threshing-floor.

It's when I sleep that I see clearly
Wild with a sweet poison,
With pearls heaped in my hands
I dwell in the heart of a seashell,
I'm the fountain down in the canyon

And the lair of the savage beast—
Or the moon as it wanes
Dying beyond the ridge.
It's when I sleep that I see clearly
Wild with a sweet poison.

I GOT TO THAT TOWN, THEY ALL GREETED ME,
AND I DIDN'T RECOGNIZE A SOUL; WHEN I
STARTED TO READ MY POEMS, THE DEVIL, LURK-
ING BEHIND A TREE, CALLED OUT TO ME, JEER-
ING, AND PILED CLIPPINGS INTO MY HANDS

What's the name of this place
With flowers all over the steeple
And dark trees by the river?
Now where did I put my keys . . .

Everyone greets me: "Good morning!"
I'm walking around in tatters;
Some of them genuflect,
Another gives me his hand.

"What's my name?" I beg them.
I stare at my naked foot;
In the shadow of a barrel
A pool of blood is shining.

A herdsman hands me a book,
I see myself there as through glass;
I'm sporting a huge beard—
Now where did I put my apron . . .

What a big crowd in the plaza!
They must be waiting for me—
Me, to read them my poems.
They laugh and drift away.

The bishop pins a cross on me.
Already the musicians have stopped.
I'd like to go back home now
But don't know all the roads here.

What if some girl kissed me . . .
What would my job be after that?
Doors are being slammed:
Who'll tell me where the inn is?

On a scrap of newspaper
My picture's blowing about;
The trees in the plaza
Are all waving goodbye.

—What's that the radio's saying?
I'm shivering, I'm scared, I'm starving;
Oh well, buy him a watch:
When did you say is his birthday?

I'm headed for Font Vella:
They've cleared away the benches;
And now I spy the Devil
Waiting for me at the corner.

September 1942

III

The Blonde on the Beach

THE BLONDE ON THE BEACH

I

You, I

You sat on the grass.
I ran about in the sun.

I brought you daisies.
He made you a daisy crown.

You made another for me.
I lay in the shade and slept.

So it was our lives were changed
when I was four years old
and you were twenty-eight.

II
The Blonde on the Beach

The Hudson's choppy today
all the way up to Troy, N.Y.
No lolling on the beaches.
There *aren't* any beaches.
    &
it's raining, raining.
And it's the next day now.
Yesterday was weary,
nothing to do, just weary
all the way up to Troy, N.Y.

Today no blonde on the beach.

                                Say that
your propellors are whirring, tailguns spitting,
joystick flipping, mania depressing:

    No blondes on the beach,
                              each
    sweeter than a peach.

It's a commuter day in old Manhattan.
It's a make-believe-ballroom day in El Salvador.
My thoughts are a bore.
They're ashamed, they're hiding
on the other side of the sheet, peep-
ing over the edge, hop-
ing they won't be noticed. Cul-
de-sac passionel du poète beachless et blondeless.

III
Old Men in Love

Nights of the full moon, rolling clouds
will come, whether we watch or sleep.

And whether it's we, or you and another,
it will be true.

And this one life—touches here, there,
all our delight, these fated shadows . . .

Old men in love: go suck your pipes
and wind your beards from neck to knees

        and hold your peace.

IV

Du im Voraus

(from the German of Rainer Maria Rilke)

You from the outset
lost beloved, my never-arrived,
I've no idea, none, what tones are dear to you.
No longer do I hope, when the moment wells up,
to recognize you. All the vast
scenes inside me, so far off, so familiar,
cities and towers and bridges and un-
foreseen winding of ways
and that stormy world where gods
once strode through the lands:
all this within me presses toward one meaning:
you, vanishing.

Oh, the gardens are you,
oh, I saw them with such
yearning. An open window
in the country-house,—and you almost stepped forth
to me, bemused. Streets I came upon,—
you had just gone down them,
and sometimes the mirrors in the shops
were still giddy with you and, startled, shot back
my too-sudden reflection.—Who knows, if the very same
bird didn't call through us both
separately, yesterday, in the evening?

43

OFFSTAGE MUSIC

I

I like those sentimental
strains of old nostalgia,

Charlie Chaplin tunes
with half-mast mustachios

tickling passing naiads,
broken shoes kicking

at some bent-over leftover
watchman at Paradise Gate,

some Keystone Kop's behind
on the Street of Lost Disillusions.

II

Too lazy to walk, the birds
are flying. Why not?
When suicide last came to mind
I was too melancholy
to *entertain* the thought.

III

The insulted and injured want
their pound of flesh, as though
all the ghosts of the world
could ever find it.—
                    Shylock,
old mathematician,
you had the right equation.
The x remains unknown.

Someone somewhere one isn't,
some girl just off to college,
new typewriter, new jeans,
beyond the haunts of the halt—
                    Shylock,
old meataphysician,
there's another right equation.
The x remains unknown.

Some kid, in morning sunlight,
thinks, "Me, walking in morning sunlight.
I'm going wherever I'm going,
choose what to do or not."—
                    Shylock,
old murder-logician,
you lost your game of position.
The x remains unknown.

46

IV

"Already the day wanes,"
laments a young man at dawn—
"and her love too is waning!"

At sunset an ardent old man
with ghost-moons and death on the brain
wonders where despair has flown.

FLURRY

It's snowing so gently today
it all vanishes as soon as seen—
but just now, abruptly,
it's slanting down harder. The wind's
blasting it every which way but mostly
seaward, where the great storms shriek
over the crashing Atlantic. Death's old
mad, first, uncaring howl still compels
the heart's return. This moment (look!)
the snow has stopped . . . except
for a few flakes on random holiday.

WHAT WE DID

"Down their carved names the rain-drop ploughs."—Hardy

We sang all the way to Indiana, we really did.
It was just an old Dodge, and when it began to rattle
my stepfather remarked, wisely: "It must be the muffler."
Mrs. Feinbaum, our family friend just turned seventy,
replied, in Yiddish: "Although I'm no expert—"
(in the inbuilt irony of Yiddish it's *"since* I'm no expert")—
"Although I'm no expert, it's my opinion
it's indeed the muffler." My mother wondered:
"Perhaps the car has run out of gas?"

So we rolled onward to—was it the dunes? Michigan City?
My half-brother Danny led the singing: multilingual:
Chicago, Boston, Cleveland, and basic Yiddish-English.
(Did you ever hear "Old MacDonald" in basic Yiddish-English?)
Before that we'd had another Dodge. It broke down once
(once?—well, only once *this* trip) on the Boston Post Road
on our way to New York. Someone came and fixed it
while we had coffee and rolls in a nearby diner.
Oh how delicious it was! I've had nothing better since!
My six-year-old tongue had never known coffee before,
not even mostly milk, and with sugar in it,
or tasted how fine life was with fresh hard rolls and butter!

And I remember the tingling winter morning
when I, a fifth grade hall-monitor, saw Danny at the door,
a beaming first grader—so happy because he saw me too—
at the head of an army of tots waiting to be let in,
and a teacher cried: "Just look at that little boy bouncing!"

KEEPING IN TOUCH

I'm hovering on the outskirts of my soul. I've
picked up a little helicopter
with a chair, a lamp, a typewriter.
                                    I've
got nothing to do but just hover
till the waiting time is over.
                        Sometimes
I see, where the angle toward Heaven is right,
a blur of (possible) light.
                        Sometimes
there's something like a flare
(I think) deep in the misty air.
                              Meanwhile
time must hold still, everywhere,
                        meanwhile . . .

NOTES

As for Love (title-sequence)
"An old man with beautiful eyes" (see "Dissolving Mirror")—the
poet Zhao Ruihong, whose poem "Souzhow Lanes in the Rain" recalls
a vanished Chinese world that has somehow attached itself to my own
memory. Certain tones and figures in *As for Love*—as in the lines be-
ginning "When I begged for bread in doorways" in "The Rose of Love
and the Lotus"—connect associatively with Zhao's poem, a translation
of which follows the sequence.

The Chinese strain in these poems reflects a compressed experience
of Chinese cities and people, and of conversations and discussions with
Chinese poets and other writers.

"As for Love"
"Are you not weary of ardent ways?"—from the villanelle in James
Joyce's *A Portrait of the Artist as a Young Man,* part 5.

"Farewell without Leaving"
Ich vill nit shtarbn!" (Yiddish)—"I *won't* die!" (or: "I don't want
to die!")

≥ ≥ ≥

"A Choice of Titles"
The quoted passages are from a televised newscast (28 March 1983)
and from Osip Mandelstam's "We Shall Die" (translated by George
Reavey).

The supernatural figures, in one early version, may be found in the
Book of Job.

53

"Golden Thoughts"
The constellation Orion has two School-of-Picasso eyes, the bright stars Rigel (blue) and Betelgeuse (red). The Pleiades (the daughters of Atlas) live in the nearby constellation Taurus. One of them is missing, and Orion has thus far refused comment.

"one poet"—See Carl Sandburg, "Grass."

Seven Poems by J. V. Foix

J. V. Foix (1894-1987) initiated—together with Joan Salvat Papasseit—the new turn of Catalan poetry in the second decade of our century. Foix belongs to the company of great modernist poets and artists.